How to Write a Press Release, Second Edition

A Beginner's Guide For Anyone Interested In Writing And Submitting Dynamite Press Releases, Including Sample Templates And Listing Of Free Press Release Distribution Services

D0449050

by

Brian Cook

Table of Contents

Introduction

A well-written press release can help your business achieve several objectives: it can generate internet publicity; it can define your message and defend your brand; it can get links with high-ranking websites; it can make your content indexable by major search engines; and it can make your message available to news outlets and thousands of RSS recipients.

Although it can seem daunting, there is no reason that any business owner cannot take advantage of the nearly free publicity offered by online press releases by easily writing and submitting one within a single day. (And, once you discover its effectiveness, you will likely begin distributing press releases on a regular basis.)

In the following pages, you will discover how to craft powerful and effective press releases; begin writing your own press release using the enclosed sample releases as a guide; and jump start your press release submissions using any of the free distribution services listed in the final chapter.

Writing Press Releases

Not too long ago, if you wanted to run a press release, you had to submit it to a media outlet--knowing that it would be accessible to readers of traditional media only for thirty days. Now, for a much lower price (often for free), your online press release is available forever to anyone on the Internet, and can include images, video, and audio.

Press releases are a great way to report on current events with your business, such as: announcements about new products; employee news; anniversaries; awards; new ventures; special offers; and many more.

When you are writing an online press release, keep in mind that you actually have two audiences... the people you want to read your announcement, AND the search engines that you want to find your press release and make it available to those people.

Follow these pointers when writing your press release:

- use a powerful opening
- use a "hook" such as tying your release to a current event
- include your website
- avoid using email addresses (prevents spambots)
- choose keywords and include them in lead sentence, headline, and summary
- write in the "third" person and limit use of jargon
- avoid the appearance of an advertisement, or using exclamation points!
- use quotes when possible
- avoid using "I", "you", or "we" outside of a quoted statement
- proofread

Now let's review the basic parts of an online press release:

Headline

- include most important keywords
- grab reader's attention
- capitalize all words except prepositions
- specify location if applicable
- no website address
- limit length (Google only allows 60 characters for headline)

Example:

XYZ Company Celebrates Over 10 Years of Department of Defense Sub-Contracting

Summary

- typically only one or two sentences
- summarize information contained in press release
- entice readers to want to read more
- include keywords

Example:

XYZ Company, Inc., a leading defense sub-contractor is celebrating its tenth year of providing aerospace flight-testing services for the U.S. Air Force and other Department of Defense clients.

Lead

- include dateline: city, state, day, month, year
- addresses the who, what, where, when, and why
- typically 30 words or less
- include keywords

Example:

Denver, Colorado, May 3, 2011 - XYZ Company, Inc., a leading defense sub-contractor, celebrates 10 years of providing aerospace flight-testing services.

Body

- about 300 to 750 words in length
- 3 or 4 sentences per paragraph max.
- include your website

- include quotes if applicable
- use final paragraph to summarize main points

Example:

Recent accomplishments for XYZ Company, Inc., (www.website.com) include completing significant upgrades for terrain-following software ahead of schedule and under cost for the U.S. Air Force, and being awarded as Colorado's Small Business of the Year (technology category).

Other recent defense contracts included an online tracking environment for the U.S. Coast Guard, several presentations for U.S. Space Command (Colorado), and missile-tracking software training for a U.S. Department of Defense client, as well as the continued development and maintenance of www.xyzsite.com for NORAD of Colorado Springs, Colorado, USA.

"Our software production and training efforts began with informal slide shows and tabletop discussions with industry leaders, and now, over 10 years later, our work includes significant and highly sensitive deliverables for the defense industry" explains XYZ Company's president, John Smith.

Boilerplate

- typically 1 or 2 sentences
- describes the basics about the company
- include services, credentials, awards, etc.
- include website

Example:

XYZ Company, Inc. maintains offices in Denver, Colorado, and Tampa, Florida and it is on the Internet at www.website.com. They are keenly positioned to provide continued sub-contract technical services that result in dynamic and cost-effective advanced for the U.S. Department of Defense on a worldwide basis.

Contact Information

- include name, title, company name, telephone, website

Example:

Contact:

Bill Smith, V.P. Marketing

XYZ Company, Inc.

(123) 456-7890

www.website.com

Sample Press Releases

One of the best ways to learn how to write an effective press release is to study "live" examples. For some up-to-the-minute releases, go to prnewswire.com or marketwire.com and select from hundreds to read from. After doing so, you will begin to get a feel for how the good ones are constructed.

Tip: Go to prweb.com and search for the type of press release you are interested in writing (i.e., "new software")... you'll get some great ideas that way!

You can also use any of the following fictional releases to help you get started writing your own:

Company Announcement

XYZ Company Celebrates Over 10 Years of Department of Defense Sub-Contracting

XYZ Company, Inc., a leading defense sub-contractor is celebrating its tenth year of providing aerospace flight-testing services for the U.S. Air Force and other Department of Defense clients.

Denver, Colorado, May 3, 2011 - XYZ Company, Inc., a leading defense sub-contractor, celebrates 10 years of providing aerospace flight-testing services.

Recent accomplishments for XYZ Company, Inc., (www.website.com) include completing significant upgrades for terrain-following software ahead of schedule and under cost for the U.S. Air Force, and being awarded as Colorado's Small Business of the Year (technology category).

Other recent defense contracts included an online tracking environment for the U.S. Coast Guard, several presentations for U.S. Space Command (Colorado), and missile-tracking software training for a U.S. Department of Defense client, as well as the continued development and maintenance of www.xyzsite.com for NORAD of Colorado Springs, Colorado, USA.

"Our software production and training efforts began with informal slide shows and tabletop discussions with industry leaders, and now, over 10 years later, our work includes significant and highly sensitive deliverables for the defense industry" explains XYZ Company's president, John Smith.

XYZ Company, Inc. maintains offices in Denver, Colorado, and Tampa, Florida and it is on the Internet at www.website.com. They are keenly positioned to provide continued sub-contract technical services that result in dynamic and cost-effective advanced for the U.S. Department of Defense on a worldwide basis.

Contact:
Bill Smith, V.P. Marketing

XYZ Company, Inc.

(123) 456-7890

www.website.com

Sports Event

Up and Coming Golf Star Enhances Spirit of Community Support to Sports Fans in Montgomery, Alabama

River Region Community Golf Event Set for Oct. 15 in Montgomery County, AL, Features TV Giveaway from BestBuy for Hole-in-One.

Montgomery, Aug. 21, 2011 — The Leadership in Golfing Foundation announces that John Smith, locally known as "JB," will be playing in Montgomery County, Alabama in his premier community-sponsored golf event on October 15, 2011. JB, 17, began golfing at the age of nine and in seven short years has grown to lead his golf demographic, winning more than 33 local and national tournaments.

JB, through sharing his talent and commitment to excellence with other young golfers just like him, hopes to encourage other to excel in both golf and school through hard work, commitment, and by supporting the community. "I invite all young golfers and golf fans of any age to join me in Alabama on Oct. 15. You will see firsthand the excitement of youth involvement in golf," said JB.

JB, poised to become a leading player on the LPGA tour, has been featured in several national magazines, including Sports Illustrated. He was also recently selected as Amateur of the Year by the Georgia Sports Council.

JB invites local businesses, major corporations, business owners, professional athletes, groups and individuals to show their support for the event and to help demonstrate the importance of providing support to local youth. "This support will help young people turn their dreams into reality. Don't miss it - and bring your family and friends with you," said JB.

Contact:
Jill Smith, Organizer
River Region Foundation

(123) 456-7890

www.website.com

Physical Fitness

Stay at Home Magazine Helps Moms Battle Weight Gain

Seven full-time stay at home moms took part in a year-long Stay Fit at Home program.

MONTGOMERY, AL, April 3, 2011 — Stress, long hours, and tight budgets leave many full time parents frustrated in their desire to lead fit, healthy lives. Nowhere is that frustration more prevalent than among stay at home moms, who typically work long hours every day, and face limited food choices combined with little opportunity for exercise.

Recognizing the struggles its stay at home moms face, Stay at Home magazine launched the Stay Fit at Home program, a year-long model designed to help them take steps to lead healthier lives. More than 250 applicants vied for entry into the program by writing an essay about why they wanted to lose weight and adopt a healthier lifestyle. The essays highlighted their years of struggling with diet and exercise and their concerns with maintaining their figures.

The seven moms chosen to participate received a free weight-loss and fitness program designed by a medical doctor to address their individual fitness needs. Beginning this month, Stay at Home magazine will follow their journey through the pages of the magazine and by website entries made by each participant. Two of moms, who are featured in the April issue of Stay at Home magazine (www.website.com) are:

— 31-year-old Kim Smith, Montgomery, AL, who has a pair of two-year old twins, and another child due soon. Her goal is to lose at least 30 pounds.

— 27-year-old Joyce Smith, Montgomery, AL, who has three boys between one and four, wants to lose 25 pounds by Christmas.

Stay at Home magazine is the largest selling publication for stay at home parents, including men and women. More than 220,000 copies of this magazine are distributed monthly to subscribers and various retail outlets.

Contact:

Kathy Smith, Editor

Stay at Home Magazine

(123) 456-7890

www.website.com

Special Offer

XYZ Company Celebrates 12th Anniversary of Internet Retail with Special Rebate Program

October special offer provides incentive for individuals and families to store up for next season's beach and other summer activities.

MONTGOMERY, AL, October 2, 2011 — Not many retailers can make the claim that they've been in business online for 12 years. But XYZ Company, (www.website.com), a well-known local company, with a national internet presence, is celebrating its 12th Anniversary of Internet-based sales this October, having first launched in October 1999.

To celebrate its landmark success, XYZ Company President, John Smith, has just announced that the company is offering its loyal customers a 25 percent rebate off all online items this month.

"When we started pursuing sales 12 years ago, we

had no idea that it would eventually overtake our retail store in terms of gross sales, Smith says. "But we've stood the 'test of time,' and come out as a leader within the outdoor activity industry. The key to our longevity remains in our ability to provide only the highest quality products at discount prices. That, and our commitment to service after the sale."

XYZ Company has solidified its position as one of the top Internet sources for individuals and various groups interested in timely-delivery of items, especially beach gear such as sunscreen, blankets, and flotation devices.

Contact:
John Smith, President
XYZ Company
(123) 456-7890
www.website.com

New Book

New Book for Entrepreneurs Features 15 High Demand Services for the B2B Community

New book, "15 Lucrative Professional Services Needed Now," provides in-depth analysis of fifteen business-to-business entrepreneurial opportunities including case studies of successful businesses.

MONTGOMERY, AL, June 3, 2011 — Recession-related layoffs and corporate hiring freezes have heightened the interest for professionals to begin successful work from home ventures. These same individuals are also understandably concerned about remaining solvent during the business start-up phase. That concern should be dispelled by "15 Lucrative Professional Services Needed Now" (www.website.com), which demonstrates that professionals can leverage their experience to successfully start home-based businesses which cater to the business community.

John Smith, the author, is a business consultant formerly with Ford and Chevron, whose background - in planning, programming, sales, and marketing - enabled him to identify the 15 opportunities he describes. While most of these businesses aren't usually thought of as home-based, he presents current day success stories of each opportunity presented.

Most of the business opportunities can be started without a specific educational background, although two of them do require a juris doctor degree. In addition, several require various certifications in addition to standard licensing requirements.

As Smith details each opportunity, readers will: learn about successful role models; understand specific entry requirements; become acquainted with typical workday activities; gain realistic income expectations; and more.

While there are many books providing work at home advice, Smith's provides up-to-date information on legitimate and lucrative entrepreneurial opportunities that professionals can pursue now.

Contact:

John Smith, Author

(123) 456-7890

www.website.com

Company Wins Award

XYZ Firm Honored with Fifth Year on INC.'s Best Companies to Work for List

Local firm selected as one of INC.'s 100 best companies to work for fifth year in a row.

MONTGOMERY, AL, Feb 18, 2011 — XYZ Firm has been honored with its 5th year on the INC.'s 2011 "100 Best Companies to Work For" list. XYZ Firm ranked 32 on the
2011 list released today. XYZ Firm is the only mental health facility in the nation to make the list for five consecutive years.

XYZ Firm was first invited to apply for selection to the INC. list in 2006 and has made the list every year since. INC. has issued the list of "100 Best Companies to Work For" since 1997. Only 3 of the original companies named to the list remain on the list in 2011 and only 23 have been on the list for five or more years.

XYZ Firm's fifth year on the list is very timely as the facility is also celebrating the 50th anniversary of its founding. XYZ Firm was founded in 1961 with the support of community leaders who were convinced that the River Region should have its own mental health facility.

"Our fifth year on the INC. list is a notable achievement that distinguishes us as a top employer," said XYZ Firm's President John Smith. "As the preferred mental health employer, XYZ Firm has the ability to attract the best providers. We consider each of our employees a caregiver committed to putting the patient first and providing the highest quality of care and service to patients and their families."

INC. selects the companies on the list based on evaluation of the policies and culture of the company and the opinions of the company's own employees. Most of the total score comes from employee responses to a confidential 47-question survey. The survey goes to several hundred randomly selected employees from each company. More than 50,000 employees from each company represented responded to the survey.

Contact:

Jim Smith, President

XYZ Firm

(123) 456-7890

www.website.com

Direct Mail Seminar

XYZ Company Debuts New Power Lunch Direct Mail Training Seminar

Nationally ranked direct mail training company launches new web-based seminars.

MONTGOMERY, AL, Oct. 4, 2011 — XYZ Company, the leader in providing direct mail training and marketing solutions for small business owners, today announced its new Power Lunch Direct Mail Training Seminar designed to teach business owners how to land more customers using tested direct mail campaigns.

The Power Lunch Direct Mail Training Seminar will be conducted via web seminars and offered free to all who wish to attend. The 30-minute sessions, which are to be held monthly, will cover everything from sales psychology, communication techniques, and preferred postcard and business letter formats. "The sessions are designed to benefit anyone who wants to increase their knowledge and understanding of how to effectively used direct mail campaigns," said Jenny Smith, President of XYZ Company.

Each session will be conducted by Smith, who has been successful in the direct mail industry since 1999. She is a nationally recognized consultant who has trained many of today's top direct mail campaign directors. She also was a featured speaker this past June at The Direct Mail Training Conference in Birmingham. "Without proper guidance and direction direct mail can be a tough market in which to succeed. To that end, we have been offering training assistance in the form of our seminar products for the past four years," said Smith.

To learn more about XYZ Company's Power Lunch Series and its full suite of web- based direct mail campaign products, visit XYZ Company at www.website.com.

Contact:
Jenny Smith, President

XYZ Company

(123) 456-7890

www.website.com

New Service

XYZCompany.com Goes Live Just as 2011 Tornado Season Threatens Intense Season

New tornado tracking website provides the latest news on Tornado Alley as major storms near the Midwest.

MONTGOMERY, AL, June 2, 2011 — Tornado storm activity has taken off the last few days ... and just in time for Midwestern residents, businesses, and tourists, there is a new website to provide current hurricane news and information. XYZ Company (www.website.com) consolidates tornado news for quick and easy reference around the clock.

"The website provides more than just tornado news; it also provides a variety of helpful internet tools," stated website owner John Smith.

Smith provides an example of how the XYZ Company website can help a family during a tornado emergency: With this website parents can have their kids track an approaching tornado with the site's reports and storm tracking maps while mom and dad learn how to protect their family, pets and property from the coming storm. They can also review shelter locations; and, after the tornado has passed, can even file a FEMA application online if need be.

"Existing web resources were either too specialized or too complex for the average homeowner or business owner in need of quick tornado information. Because of that, this website was specifically designed to be more useful by individuals, families and businesses reacting to a tornado or other disasters," said Smith.

As the name implies, XYZ Company is not just for tornados, but for many types of disasters. It can be considered a directory of disaster-related information because it consolidates news and information on many natural and man-made disasters, such as hurricanes, earthquakes, floods, and even the flu.

XYZ Company (www.website.com) is a disaster information website that provides one-stop access for disaster news, resources, and help with FEMA around the clock. XYZ Company was designed by a tornado expert with over 15 years of experience in disaster relief.

Contact:

John Smith, Owner

XYZ Company

(123) 456-7890

www.website.com

Entertainment

XYZ Company Introduces Future Stars with Top Entertainment Icons

XYZ Company reports over ninety percent success rate for linking event participants with entertainment industry talent.

MONTGOMERY, AL, Dec. 28, 2011 — In the entertainment industry, it is definitely who you know. And the success of XYZ Company's (www.website.com) recent networking event definitely proves that saying true. The program, which took place Nov. 30, 2011, at Montgomery's Shakespeare Festival, featured a day packed with entertainment industry-achievement stories, seminars, and career advice offered by some of the industry's most notable superstars.

"Talent and ambition alone often aren't enough to propel you toward success in the entertainment industry," says Kim Smith, XYZ Company's director.

"Through XYZ Company's unique networking events, we're providing qualified individuals with firsthand insight on how to get their "big break". We're also providing the opportunity to meet personally with highly successful entertainers."

Since launching the first XYZ Company event in January of this year, the company has already held three events across the South. Participation by notables in the entertainment industry has increased twofold, and is projected to be even greater at the next XYZ Company event, which takes place in Atlanta, Georgia, on Feb. 3, 2012.

"The main thing is really the networking, considering that everyone attending is making crucial contacts," Smith says. "People work for years to land a conversation with insiders, but we literally make that connection happen at XYZ Company events. Perhaps most exciting is the fact that one in every ten attendees will land a huge opportunity."

From dancing, acting, and music, XYZ Company is

all about trying to find tomorrow's big entertainment stars. As a network marketing company, XYZ Company puts its clients together with some of the industry's biggest names.

Contact:
Kim Smith, Director
XYZ Company
(123) 456-7890
www.website.com

Pets

Local Montgomery Author Writes Statewide Animal Shelter Guide

New book, "Alabama Pet Rescue Shelters," provides detailed contact information on over one hundred animal rescue shelters located within Alabama.

MONTGOMERY, AL, Nov.12, 2011 — Local author Steve Smith has published a new book outlining information about each of the state's animal rescue shelters.

Animal lovers know the dilemma - they often want to help care for rescue animals but can't always find current, accurate information for their region. Steve Smith, a retired Air Force officer, knows the problem well. "My wife and I have a real heart for golden retrievers, but we couldn't always locate current information about these dogs in a way that we could take action. Now we have provided a resource that people can use to get more involved in the animal rescue process" he says.

As Smith began researching the shelters that existed in Alabama, he discovered that trying to find pertinent facts regarding shelter locations, hours, types of animals, and so on, was difficult at best. As a result, all of his notes on the topic eventually made their way into a book, "Alabama Pet Rescue Shelters."

Smith has created what amounts to a pet lover's guide to finding animals in the state that need help now. The book also references a website (www.website.com) which Smith has developed to complement the book and provide updates as needed.

Smith also founded the RescuePet Foundation (www.website.com), a private, not- for-profit, tax-exempt organization that accepts donations for assisting Alabama animal rescue shelters in emergencies.

Contact:

Steve Smith, Author

(123) 456-7890

www.website.com

Free Press Release Services

Using any of the top paid online press release services, such as prnewswire.com, marketwire.com, and prweb.com, can be very effective when used correctly. However, if cost is an issue, you can often get good results by submitting your press releases to free press release outlets such as the ones listed below. (You might want to start with these regardless as you hone your press release writing skills).

http://www.pressreleasepoint.com

http://www.pr-usa.net

http://www.prfocus.com

http://www.anyrelease.com

http://www.prurgent.com

http://www.prlog.com

http://www.pressexposure.com

http://www.free-press-release.com

http://www.pressreleasespider.com

http://www.pagerelease.com

http://www.bignews.biz

http://www.nationalprwire.com

http://www.free-news-release.com

http://www.pressrelease.com

http://www.pr9.net

http://www.i-newswire.com

http://www.clickpress.com

http://www.freepressindex.com

http://www.openpr.com

http://www.ecommwire.com

http://www.24-7pressrelease.com

Finally, if you are interested in automating the submission of your releases to many of the free press release outlets, you may want to consider purchasing "PressBot", by IncanSoft.com, or other similar software to save you time when submitting press releases on a frequent basis.

New..."Local Web Secrets: A Guide to Starting and Running a Profitable Local Website"

You're about to discover why local websites are among the quickest and easiest ways to create a real online business, and how to get one started successfully in less time, and for far less money, than you might imagine.

Online entrepreneurs often struggle when trying to create a profitable website. This book shows you how to start an easy online business, and gives you what you need to start making money quickly, without a lot of hype or ridiculous promises. It's over 100 pages of practical "how to," and dozens of resources you can use to cut your learning time, and your costs, to the bone.

Get more information at:
http://www.localwebsecrets.com or search for "Local Web Secrets" on Amazon.com.

Made in the USA
San Bernardino, CA
05 December 2013